Superstar Cars

Mustang

Lynn Peppas

CRABTREE
Publishing Company
www.crabtreebooks.com

Superstar Cars

Author: Lynn Peppas
Publishing plan research and development:
  Sean Charlebois, Reagan Miller
  Crabtree Publishing Company
Editor: Sonya Newland
Proofreader: Molly Aloian
Editorial director: Kathy Middleton
Project coordinator and prepress technician: Margaret Salter
Print coordinator: Katherine Berti
Series consultant: Petrina Gentile
Cover design: Ken Wright
Design: Simon Borrough
Photo research: Amy Sparks

Photographs:
Alamy: Transtock Inc. p. 1, 26, 28–29, 31, 32, 34–35, 48, 52;
  picturesbyrob: p. 16–17; Paul Broadbent: p. 27; Alvey &
  Towers Picture Library: p. 45; Performance Image: p. 46;
  Will Newitt: p. 54; Mark Scheuern: p. 58
Corbis: H. Armstrong Roberts: p. 5; Bettmann: p. 9;
  R. Krubner/ClassicStock: p. 21
Ford: p. 7, 8, 10, 11, 12, 13, 18, 19, 20, 22, 23, 24, 25, 30, 33, 34
  (left), 36, 37, 38–39, 39 (right), 40–41, 42–43, 43 (top), 44, 47,
  50, 51, 53, 55, 56, 57, 59
Motoring Picture Library: p. 6, 14, 49; Tom Wood: p. 15
Shutterstock: front cover; 6th Gear Advertising: p. 4.

Library and Archives Canada Cataloguing in Publication

Peppas, Lynn
      Mustang / Lynn Peppas.

(Superstar cars)
Includes index.
Issued also in an electronic format.
ISBN 978-0-7787-2145-1 (bound).--ISBN 978-0-7787-2152-9 (pbk.)

      1. Mustang automobile--Juvenile literature.
I. Title. II. Series: Superstar cars

TL215.M8P46 2011   j629.222'2   C2010-905625-6

Library of Congress Cataloging-in-Publication Data

Peppas, Lynn.
      Mustang / Lynn Peppas.
            p. cm. -- (Superstar cars)
      Includes index.
      ISBN 978-0-7787-2152-9 (pbk. : alk. paper) --
      ISBN 978-0-7787-2145-1 (reinforced library binding : alk. paper) --
      ISBN 978-1-4271-9550-0 (electronic (pdf))
      1. Mustang automobile--Juvenile literature. I. Title. II. Series.

TL215.M8P47 2010
629.222'2--dc22

2010034932

Crabtree Publishing Company

www.crabtreebooks.com   1-800-387-7650

Printed in the U.S.A./102010/SP20100915

Published in Canada
Crabtree Publishing
616 Welland Ave.
St. Catharines, ON
L2M 5V6

Published in the United States
Crabtree Publishing
PMB 59051
350 Fifth Avenue, 59th Floor
New York, New York 10118

Published in the United Kingdom
Crabtree Publishing
Maritime House
Basin Road North, Hove
BN41 1WR

Published in Australia
Crabtree Publishing
386 Mt. Alexander Rd.
Ascot Vale (Melbourne)
VIC 3032

❯ Contents

Chapter 1

Mustang Mania

The mustang, a small but sturdy wild horse found on America's western plains, has run free since its ancestors arrived with the first Spanish settlers. Mustangs, often called ponies because of their size, embody the beauty, freedom, and spirit of America.

Spirit of America

In 1964, the living symbol of the free spirit gave its name to a mechanical one when the Ford Motor Company released its first Ford Mustang **production car**. Like its namesake, the car was small, dependable, and could run like the wind. Since its release nearly 50 years ago, the Mustang has become one of the best-loved and most popular American cars.

Mustangs have been around for nearly half a century. Even after all these years, the modern cars still have a family resemblance.

What's in a name?

Nobody knows for sure whose idea it was to name Ford's new sports car the Mustang. However, it is known that the name had been used at the company before 1964—an earlier Ford two-seater **concept car** had been called Mustang, but it was never **mass-produced**.

Birth of a legend

Some people say that the name was thought up by one of Ford's stylists, Pres Harris, who admired the P-51 Mustang, a World War II fighter plane. Others say that Ford's market-research manager Bob Eggert—who raised horses as a hobby—came up with the name.

Whatever the case, Mustang was one of six names that ended up on a list prepared by John Conley, who worked for Ford's advertising agency. He presented the list to Henry Ford II, Lee Iacocca, and other Ford **executives**. Although some of them originally preferred the name Cougar, they all eventually agreed to call the new car the Mustang.

Mustang music

Mustangs have captured the imagination of popular American musicians. Among the songs whose lyrics reflect the car's popularity is "Mustang Sally," a hit sung by the country and western singer Wilson Pickett in the mid-1960s. It's not just older music that celebrates the Mustang, though. The rock band Five for Fighting have a song called "'65 Mustang," which was released in 2006.

The first production Mustang rolled off the assembly line at Dearborn, Michigan, on March 9, 1964.

>> What is a pony car?

Mustangs belong to a group of vehicles called pony cars. This is an American term that describes a small, affordable, sporty, two-door car that can seat up to four people. In terms of style, pony cars can be recognized by their long front ends and shorter rear ends.

Small but sporty

The term "pony car" was first coined by American car-magazine editor Dennis Shattuck. He felt that the Ford Mustang epitomized this new breed of small but speedy cars, so he referred to them as pony cars. The name stuck, and today this type of car is still called a pony car.

Other pony cars

Several other cars were classified as pony cars, including the Plymouth Barracuda and the Chevrolet Camaro. In fact, the Barracuda went on sale to the public before the Ford Mustang. In this way the importance of the Mustang speaks for itself. Small four-seater sports cars are classified as "pony cars" rather than being called "fish cars" after the Barracuda!

> "Pony car" was the perfect term for a sporty car that was smaller than many of its competitors.

Mustang takes the lead

Mustang took the lead in pony-car sales early on, largely due to its reputation for combining a sporty look with a very affordable price.

In 1965, Ford produced over 681,000 Mustangs. In that same year, Plymouth produced just over 64,000 Barracudas, the Mustang's main competitor (the Barracuda had come on the market in 1964). Another famous American sports car, the Chevrolet Corvette, only sold 24,000 cars in 1965. In fact, it took Corvette 25 years to reach the 500,000 mark in sales—and this was still fewer cars than the Mustang had sold in its first year!

Lasting success

More than 45 years later, Mustangs have kept their reputation for being sporty, dependable, and affordable. Today, they are still one of the top-selling sports cars in America, and more people have owned a Mustang than any other single pony car around.

Galloping emblem

The graceful design of the galloping mustang horse has been the Ford Mustang's **emblem** since the car was launched. The logo was first sketched by Ford designer Philip Thomas Clark in the early 1960s. The logo has undergone a few small changes over the years, but it has appeared on Mustangs throughout their whole existence.

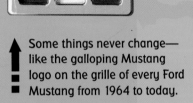

Some things never change—like the galloping Mustang logo on the grille of every Ford Mustang from 1964 to today.

7

Chapter 2

Mustang's Runaway Success

Henry Ford changed the way people traveled when he created the Model T car in 1908. Five years later, he began mass production of the car at Ford's first assembly-line plant in Highland Park, Michigan. This is where the Ford Motor Company began.

Henry Ford (here with his famous Model T) was born in Dearborn, Michigan – the same city where the Ford Mustang would be first assembled over 100 years later.

Handing over the reins

Henry's eldest grandson, Henry Ford II, was in charge of the Ford Motor Company in 1945, the year his grandfather retired. He was still running the company when the new Mustang was released in 1964. People who worked for Ford at the time said that

Henry Ford II was nervous about the new car—but he didn't need to be. People were crazy about the styling and price. It became one of the all-time success stories for the Ford Motor Company. It has also been one of the company's longest-manufactured models.

The Father of Mustang

Lee Iacocca is often called the Father of Mustang. He was vice president of Ford's car and truck division in 1964, and he felt that this was the perfect time to release a new car.

Iacocca figured that some of the first baby boomers were just turning 18 years old. He thought that they would be looking to buy a compact, youthful-looking, sporty car. He also knew that most of them would not have a lot of money to spend, so the price of the car would need to be as low as possible. He also bet on the fact that they might be thinking of starting families soon, so he made it a four-seater.

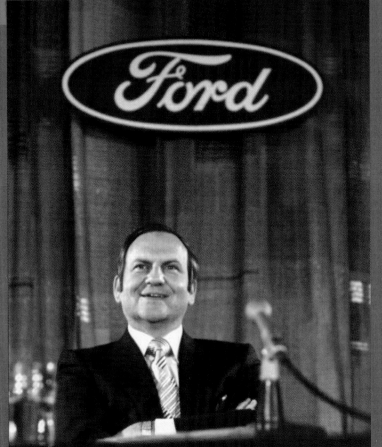

Lee Iacocca had a degree in engineering, but his real interest was in business and sales. It was his idea for Ford designers and engineers to work on creating the new car that became the Mustang.

▓ AMAZING FACTS

Record sale

Iacocca's ideas were right on the money. In its first year of sales, the Ford Mustang set a record for the highest car sales ever. Lee knew what the majority of people were looking for in a car—and it was called the Ford Mustang!

Watching costs

It is expensive to create all-new parts for a car. To help keep the price of the Mustang as low as possible, Ford's engineers used as many parts as they could from other Ford models, including the Falcon and Fairlane. Mustangs were also built in the same plant as the Falcon, in Dearborn, Michigan.

AMAZING FACTS

Midget Mustang

Mustang mania reached all Americans—even children. In 1964, a toy company created a children's-sized, push-pedal Mustang look-alike called the Midget Mustang. This toy sold for US$12.95, which would be worth about US$100 today.

Spare parts

The Ford Falcon was a small car, and several of its parts were used in the Mustang, including the **chassis**. Standard Mustangs were also given the same straight-six engine found in the Falcon. The optional engine was the same as the Falcon's, too—the small-block V8.

Unlike the Falcon, the Mustang was given four **torque** boxes, a feature it shared with the Ford Fairlane model. These made the Mustang sturdier, absorbed some of the shocks while driving, and gave it better handling.

This drawing shows one of the first Mustangs. It is dated 1962, two years before the Mustang was released.

Individual styling

The Mustang may have shared many of the Falcon's internal parts, but the similarities ended there. The Mustang was an entirely different car on the outside. To begin with, it was much sportier-looking than the Falcon and it sat lower to the ground. The interior of the Mustang was also very different. The Mustang was much more luxurious than the Falcon. Styling features included **bucket seats**, a vinyl interior, and carpeting.

Mustangs produced before August 1964 are often called 1964½, although Ford officially calls all cars produced from 1964 to 1965 the 1965 model.

1964½ Mustang

In the 1960s, most new car models were released in the fall before the model year. For example, a 1965 model would be released in the fall of 1964. The first production Mustangs were released in the spring of 1964—half a year later than other 1964 models had been released. For this reason, many Mustang owners whose cars were made in the spring of 1964 call their cars the 1964½ model!

11

At the 1964 World's Fair, visitors could sit inside a moving Mustang while listening to information about human achievement on the radio in one of four languages.

➤➤ Ford's star is born

The Mustang's spring release helped Ford sell more cars. In the fall, all the new car models compete against each other for buyers' attention. When the Mustang came out in the spring, it did not face the same competition and grabbed everyone's attention.

Americans first saw the Ford production Mustang during the New York World's Fair in 1964, an event designed to celebrate human achievement. Even Disney jumped onboard, offering rides on its Magic Skyway conveyor system in white Mustang convertibles.

1965 Mustang

Production years: 1964
No. built: 418,000
Top speed: 128 mph (207 km/h)
Engine type: Straight-6
Engine size: 170 ci (2.8 liter),
    101 hp
Cylinders: 6
Transmission: 3-speed automatic
    or manual, 4-speed optional
CO_2 emissions: N/A
EPA fuel economy ratings: N/A
Price: US$2,370

■ From April until August of 1964, two styles
of Mustang were offered: the **coupe** and the
convertible. After August 1964, Ford added
the 2+2 fastback Mustang to the line-up.

Global advertising

Ford made extra sure that they had
everyone's attention by advertising
the Mustang in television commercials
at the same time on all three major
American networks—ABC, NBC, and
CBS—the evening before the car's
release. On the day that the World's Fair
opened, full-page ads for the Mustang
ran in all major newspapers across the
U.S. *Newsweek* and *Time* magazines ran
cover stories on the Mustang, too.

A hit on their hands

Mustang advertising did its job—and
did it very well. People bought every
Mustang there was to be had and
ordered more that hadn't been made
yet! On the weekend that Mustangs
hit the dealerships, some reported
having to close their doors because
there were just too many people there
to see the new car.

Chapter 3

Mustang's Early Years ≫ ≫ ≫

In its first two years, the Mustang sold more cars than even Lee Iacocca had dreamed it would. At this time, the famous racecar driver Carroll Shelby (see page 44), began his long association with Mustang, creating high-performance versions such as the GT350 and GT500 models. Ford was pleased with the success— but it soon began to face competition in the pony-car class.

Competition

In 1967, General Motors (GM), Ford's biggest competitor, introduced two pony cars—the Firebird and the Camaro—to its lineup; the race to sell more pony cars was on. After Mustang's first two record-breaking years in production, sales began to decline. Ford kept its pony alive by making some changes to stay ahead of the race.

In 1966, when the Mustang **fastback** was released, sales were still high. They began to drop the following year.

Mustang builds muscle

One of the problems Ford faced was that the Mustang did not appeal to **muscle-car** enthusiasts. A muscle car is simply a small car with a big engine, and the fashion for muscle cars was at its very peak in America during the mid-1960s. To keep up with the times, in 1967, Ford decided to offer more muscular options for its Mustangs.

AMAZING FACTS

Not a Mustang?

When was a Mustang not a Mustang? When it was exported to Germany! From 1964 to 1976, the Mustang was called the T-5 in Germany. A truck company called Krupp owned the rights to the Mustang name up until December 1978.

■ The Mustang began as a small car, but through the late 1960s, it grew in size to accommodate bigger engines.

Endless options

Soon, the Mustang offered buyers more options on a car than ever before. New to the 1967 option list were two big-block V8 engines. Big-block engines were larger, and more powerful in terms of **horsepower**. In 1968 alone, buyers could choose from eight different engines to put into one of nine different styles of Mustang. Prices varied according to the style and engine size, so this might have helped a buyer make a decision!

Bigger engines meant bigger cars. By 1973, the Mustang was almost seven inches (18 cm) wider and almost one foot (31 cm) longer than the first model. It also weighed over 500 pounds (227 kg) more!

The "Bond"-able Mustang

The Mustang got its first starring role in the famous James Bond movie "Goldfinger," released in January 1965 in the United States. The car was used in a chase scene. In the scene, James Bond is driving an Aston Martin DB5 in hot pursuit of a white convertible Mustang being driven by a beautiful blonde spy.

End of the first generation

Bigger doesn't always mean better, though. Sales were dropping as quickly as the Mustang grew in size. In 1968, Semon "Bunkie" Knudsen was made president of Ford. Knudsen liked big cars and gave the Mustang a style makeover in 1969. It looked more like a muscle car, with a longer, heavier-looking hood. There were also four head-lights instead of two on the new-look vehicle. In 1969, Ford also offered special edition Mustangs—such as the Boss 302 and Boss 429—with performance engines.

During its first generation and the muscle-car era, the Mustang grew considerably larger. This is a Super Cobra 1973 muscle car.

Welcome to the 1970s

American attitudes toward cars changed with the new decade. People were less concerned with gas-guzzling speed and more concerned about protecting the environment against harmful **emissions** from car exhausts. Big-block engines generated larger amounts of harmful emissions than smaller engines. Large engines were going out of style—and quickly.

In 1963, the U.S. government enacted several laws, among them the Clean Air Act, to help control air pollution. In 1970, the government added a law that stated that all new cars produced by 1975 had to cut harmful emissions by 90 percent.

Mustang generations

Most car models are either updated with a new design or discontinued after about a ten-year run. Not many last as long as the Mustang, and it is Ford's longest-running model in America. In over 45 years there have been many changes in looks and style. Some car models mark generations in terms of style, but Mustang generations are marked by new chassis.

Oil crisis

In October 1973, the United States had an oil crisis when the Organization of Arab Petroleum Exporting Countries (OPEC) placed an oil **embargo** on the U.S. OPEC's refusal to sell oil to the United States created an oil and gasoline shortage there. Suddenly Americans were looking to buy fuel-efficient cars with smaller engines that would save on gas rather than using it up on great bursts of speed. Ford's response was to create a new generation of Mustang called the Mustang II.

The second generation

By 1970, Lee Iacocca had become unhappy with how big the Mustang had grown, so he asked his engineers and designers to return the pony car to its original, smaller size. In 1974, Ford came out with a brand-new, second-generation Mustang that was lighter and smaller than ever before. This was the Mustang II.

Ford's advertising slogan, "The right car at the right time," rang true. It was indeed the perfect time to release the compact, fuel-efficient vehicle. As the oil crisis worsened in America, people were looking to buy fuel-efficient cars.

Small engine

Along with the Mustang II's smaller size came smaller engines, too. A four-cylinder inline engine came as standard, but there was the option of upgrading to a V6. However, some Mustang owners were unhappy with exchanging power for fuel efficiency, so a year later Ford brought back the V8 engine as an option.

Ghia Mustangs

In 1970, Ford bought an Italian car company called Ghia. It was a Ghia-designed car that gave Ford designers some of their styling ideas for the Mustang II. When the Mustang II came out in 1974, a Ghia deluxe edition was also released. The popular Ghia Mustang came with a vinyl roof, wood-tone interior accents, and shag carpeting.

■ Ghia editions featured vinyl rooftops and small, rectangular side windows that were known as opera windows.

The 1974 Mustang notchback coupe style featured a vertical back window and a trunk in the rear.

1974 types

For the 1974 Mustang, only the coupe and fastback styles were offered. The convertible had been discontinued partly because of new U.S. government crash standards. In 1977, a new T-bar roof option was offered for the 2+2 hatchback version.

In its first year of sales, the Mustang II was another hit for Lee Iacocca. During the second generation's debut year, the Mustang II sold almost 386,000 cars.

Vital Statistics

1974 Mustang

Production years: 1974
No. built: 386,000
Top speed: 99 mph (159 km/h)
Engine type: Inline (I-4)
Engine size: 140 ci (2.3 liter), 88 hp
Cylinders: 4
Transmission: 3-speed automatic or 4-speed manual
CO_2 emissions: N/A
EPA fuel economy ratings: N/A
Price: US$3,134

Slowing to a trot

A more subtle change to the Mustang in 1974 could be seen in the running-horse emblem found on all Mustang II front **grilles**. The logo was redesigned, and instead of being shown at a full-out gallop, the Mustang was slowed to a trot. This made sense because the cars' engines were smaller and were not as fast, to conserve gas.

Welcome to the 1980s

The North American gas shortages that began in the 1970s carried on into the 1980s. The North American economy was in a **recession**. Commerce slowed, and many people were having a hard time. Many American businesses were affected, particularly the carmakers. A second oil crisis in 1979, sometimes called an energy crisis, cut oil **exports** to the U.S. even more. For North Americans, this meant that the cost of goods went up because oil was so expensive. Many Americans lost their jobs as a result.

AMAZING FACTS

Mustang logo move

The emblem of the running Mustang horse was located on the front grilles of the cars in the first and second generations. For the third generation, however, it was moved off the grille and onto the hood.

The second-generation Mustang Cobra was released in 1976.

During the energy crisis in America, long lines at the gas pumps were a familiar scene.

Foreign competitors

In the late 1970s, American carmakers faced another problem. Competition from foreign carmakers was cutting into their sales. Companies such as Toyota were producing smaller, fuel-efficient cars, and about 23 percent of American car-buyers were purchasing them. Ford decided that it was time, once again, to redesign its Mustang and get its pony car back into the consumer race.

Fired or retired?

Even though he was made president of Ford in 1970, Lee Iacocca only kept the job until October 15, 1977. On the very date of his fifty-fourth birthday, he officially retired from Ford. According to Iacocca himself, though, he was fired from Ford by his longtime employer, Henry Ford II. He didn't stay retired for long, moving on to become chairman of Chrysler in 1978.

The third generation

The second-generation Mustang II design lasted only five years before it was replaced by the third generation in 1979. The third generation enjoyed a longer run. Its fifteen years makes it the longest-running generation to date.

■ Ford's desire to enhance the car's aerodynamics and improve its fuel efficiency led to the changes in the third-generation Mustang.

Work on the third-generation Mustang began in 1975, just after the second generation had been released. The focus was on fuel efficiency, much as it had been for the second generation. The Mustang II's small size made the car economical, but many people felt it was cramped and lacked a certain degree of comfort! For the third generation, instead of decreasing the car's size for economy, Ford looked into changing the car's **aerodynamics** to save on gas.

Jack Telnack

Ever since he was a little boy, Jack Telnack had wanted to work for Ford. His father had worked there, and after Jack received his degree in design, he achieved his dream and got a job at Ford. In 1975, Telnack and his design team were responsible for the winning look of the third-generation Mustang. In 1987, Telnack was made Ford's vice president of design. He retired in 1997.

Third-generation models had a new chassis, called the Fox chassis, which was used on several Ford models.

Lightening the load

Another idea to give the Mustang better gas mileage was to make it lighter. The Ford engineers' solution was to use more plastic, aluminum, and other lightweight materials and to put in thinner, stronger windows. Even though it was bigger than the Mustang II, the third generation of Mustang weighed about 200 pounds (91 kg) less.

Foxy Mustang

One of the biggest changes seen in the third generation was the addition of a brand-new chassis, called the Fox chassis. "Fox" had been the code name used for the project while the chassis was being designed. The Fox chassis was eventually used in several Ford vehicles, including the Mustang, Fairmont, and Thunderbird models.

1979 styles

Three body styles were offered for the 1979 Mustang—the hardtop coupe, the **notchback**, and the hatchback. The standard engine was still the straight-line overhead camshaft (OHC) inline-4, but a new **turbocharged** option was added that boosted the Mustang's power. Other engines, including V6 and V8 models, were also offered.

■ The third generation of Mustang is often called the Fox generation. Even though it was a bigger car, it weighed less and saved more fuel than the much smaller Mustang 11.

1979 Mustang

Production years: 1979
No. built: Unknown
Top speed: Unknown
Engine type: Overhead camshaft (OHC) inline-4 (I-4)
Engine size: 2.3 liters, 131 hp
Cylinders: 4
Transmission: 4-speed manual; 3-speed automatic (standard); 5-speed manual (optional)
CO_2 emissions: N/A
EPA fuel economy ratings: N/A
Price: US$4,494 (coupe)

No coffee served at this CAFE

CAFE is an **acronym** that stands for Corporate Average Fuel Economy. In 1975, a new federal law required new vehicles to meet a standard of fuel efficiency. It set the minimum number of miles a vehicle in each size should travel on a gallon of gas. If a vehicle fell short of the standard, the carmaker had to pay a fine.

The 1983 Mustang was offered in convertible and coupe styles. The convertible was made by cutting the roof off the coupe!

Third-generation changes

Throughout its third generation, Mustang made changes to keep up with the competition. Even though many people were looking for smaller and more fuel-efficient cars, there were still some drivers who wanted more power in their pony car. Carmakers at Ford were concerned about getting the best gas mileage possible for their vehicles because of the CAFE standards. They brought in new, larger engines for their Mustangs that included a five-liter V8 but were careful to keep within CAFE standards.

Convertibles and coupes

In 1981, Mustang added the T-top roof to the Mustang lineup. This roof had not been offered since the 1978 model. The convertible style was also brought back in 1983. This style had been absent from Mustangs since 1973.

Ford made the convertible by cutting the roof off already-produced 1983 Mustang coupes. Convertible lovers were happy to see its return, and more than 20,000 convertibles were sold that year!

In 1987, Ford updated the look of the Mustang. The car became more rounded in style, with fewer sharp angles.

Facelift features

By 1986, the third generation of Mustang had kept the same look for eight model years. Ford figured it was time for a facelift; so in 1987, a new-look Mustang was unveiled. Since it was more aero-dynamic in design than previous models had been, the new look was called the aero-design. The front body was more rounded than before and featured wraparound headlights.

The rounded aero-design lasted on the Mustang until the third generation ended in 1993.

1987 styles

In 1987, the V6 engine was dropped from the options Ford offered on the Mustang. There were now two choices— the standard four-cylinder overhead camshaft engine and a new and very popular fuel-injected V8 with 225 hp.

Anniversary edition

Mustang celebrated its twenty-fifth anniversary in 1990. Mustangs produced between April 17, 1989, and April 17, 1990, had a badge on the dashboard that read "25 Years." Special anniversary editions were emerald green with white convertible ragtops. The color combination was originally dreamed up for a 7UP soda commercial. When 7UP decided not to make the commercial, the color combination went to adorn the anniversary-edition Mustang.

Maz-tangs mistake

Ford teamed up with the Japanese carmaker Mazda, with the idea of jointly designing a new Mustang. Mustang enthusiasts complained to Ford when they found out. One reason that people liked the Mustang so much was that it had an all-American image. So in 1989, Ford released the jointly designed car with a new name: the Ford Probe.

AMAZING FACTS

Officer Mustang

How do those officers in blue catch the bad guys in fast cars? In faster cars, of course! In 1982, Ford Mustang produced a specially equipped Mustang V8 notchback coupe designed to meet the needs of officers of the California Highway Patrol.

The Ford Probe began life as a collaboration between Ford and Mazda to create a new Mustang. The partnership didn't work out.

Chapter 4

The Evolution of Mustang

Mustang sales fell slowly but steadily through the 1980s and into the 1990s. The Mustang had been in competition with GM's answer to a pony car, the Camaro, since 1967. When the fourth-generation Camaro was released in 1993, Ford realized that the Mustang needed a new look to keep up with the competition.

Decisions about the future

Ford executives had been watching sales carefully, trying to decide whether to keep the Mustang line going or discontinue it altogether. In 1992, sales slipped to a record low. Fewer than 80,000 Mustangs were produced, a number that was far below the figures of prior production years. Executives knew that if sales didn't start improving soon, they would have to put the American pony out to pasture for good. They decided to give the Mustang one last shot.

One more chance

The result was revealed in 1994, with the release of the fourth-generation Mustang. People loved the new look—often because it reminded them of the classic Mustangs. People buy what they love, and sales started to increase. The fifth-generation Mustang, launched in 2005, followed the same idea and proved to be a winning formula once again. The Mustang had been saved, but not without great effort on the part of Ford's designers and engineers.

The fourth generation was a big hit with Mustang enthusiasts and car buyers. In its second year (1995), over 185,000 Mustangs were produced.

The fourth generation

Mustang's design team came up with three different styles for the fourth generation. A tame-looking model was nicknamed Bruce Jenner, after a popular American athlete. A mean-looking model was called Rambo, after the Vietnam War veteran character played by actor Sylvester Stallone. The third design, between tame and mean, was called Arnold Schwarzenegger, after the actor (he later became the governor of California). The Schwarzenegger design was the one chosen.

Sporty No. 95

A team of Ford engineers and designers had actually started working on a new generation for the Mustang in 1989—five years before the fourth generation was eventually unveiled. The engineers and designers called it the SN95, which stood for "sporty North American version no. 95."

>> Buyer's choice

Ford got some ideas for the fourth generation by **surveying** Mustang owners to find out what they would like to see in a new Mustang. Many said they wanted a dependable V8 engine, modern styling that had a hint of **retro** to it, a lot of options, and all for an affordable price. Ford carmakers went back to the drawing board to create a fourth-generation Mustang that had all these qualities.

Mystic Mustang

In 1996, a new paint color was offered as a special option for Mustang Cobra coupes. It was called "mystic." A Mystic Mustang changed from green to purple to bronze, depending on how the light was shining on it. Only 1,999 of these special-edition Mustangs were produced.

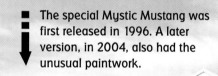
The special Mystic Mustang was first released in 1996. A later version, in 2004, also had the unusual paintwork.

Modifications

Engineers modified the original Fox chassis to improve its stiffness and to give the car better handling. The new chassis was called the Fox-4 and was two inches (five cm) longer and wider than the original Fox chassis. The bigger chassis also cut down on noise and vibration. Fourth-generation Mustangs came in two styles: notchback coupe and convertible. The hatchback was discontinued.

The emblem of a running Mustang pony was returned to the car's front grille, where it had been for the Mustang's first two generations.

◼ With the new OHC V8 engine, the GT Coupe Mustang could do 0 to 60 mph (97 km/h) in 5.9 seconds.

Vital Statistics

1996 Mustang GT

Production years: 1996
No. built: 135,620
Top speed: 152 mph (245 km/h)
Engine type: Overhead camshaft (OHC) V8
Engine size: 305 ci (5 liters), 225 hp
Cylinders: 8
Transmission: 5-speed manual
CO_2 emissions: 9.8 tons/yr
EPA fuel economy ratings: 16 mpg (city); 25 mpg (highway)
Price: US$17,610

Mustang motor mods

In 1996, Mustang made big changes to its engines when it retired the long-time OHV (overhead valve) V8 engine. These were replaced with OHC (overhead camshaft) 4.6-liter modular V8 engines. An overhead camshaft is a shaft that rotates. A cam is a solid bump on the shaft. When the shaft turns, these bumps push the valves open. The camshaft system uses fewer moving parts than the older OHV system and is more efficient.

Modular engines

The new engine that appeared from 1996 was called "modular" because it shared many of its standard-sized parts with other Ford OHC engines. The new engine was easier to put together, as the assembly line could be easily switched to produce a different engine within the same OHC family.

The OHC V8 engine has been used in other Ford vehicles, too, including the Explorer and the Thunderbird. The new engine was offered in Mustangs because the OHV V8 did not meet emissions standards, whereas the OHC V8 did.

Mustang's many homes

It was in Dearborn, Michigan, that the very first Mustang rolled off a Ford assembly line. Dearborn was also the birthplace of the Ford Motor Company's founder, Henry Ford. The assembly plant was called the Ford River Rouge Complex.

That very first Mustang came off the Dearborn assembly line on March 9, 1964. All in all, more than 8,000 Mustangs were made ready for the April 17, 1964, release date. To keep up with the first-year demand, other plants were opened in places such as San José, California, and Metuchen, New Jersey. In addition, the Shelby Mustangs were built in Las Vegas. But by 1992, Mustangs were being built in Dearborn once again. The fourth generation was the last to be constructed here though.

For the 1996 Mustang, Ford introduced a new engine—the OHC (overhead camshaft) V8, which was used in several other Ford models.

Millions of Mustangs

On November 18, 2003, the three-millionth Mustang was produced at Dearborn. It was a 2004 fortieth-anniversary crimson red GT convertible. Six months later the plant was shut down. The last car came off the assembly line there on May 10, 2004—a red Mustang GT convertible. Mustang's next generation would be built in a new home.

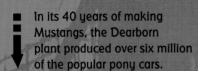

In its 40 years of making Mustangs, the Dearborn plant produced over six million of the popular pony cars.

AutoAlliance International

Since 2005, all Ford Mustangs have had a new hometown in Flat Rock, Michigan. The assembly plant is called AutoAlliance International and is shared with the Japanese carmaker Mazda. The plant is almost three million square feet (278,709 sq m) in size. The interior space is so huge that almost 47 American football fields could fit inside the plant.

>> Driving on the edge

In 1999, the Mustang received another facelift for its thirty-fifth anniversary. The new style was called the New Edge design and was one that Jack Telnack and his team had dreamed up just before Telnack retired in 1997. Where the fourth-generation Mustangs had been more rounded (described as the "jellybean" look), the new facelift featured harder, meaner-looking edges where the curves had been.

Retro dash

The fifth-generation Mustang's dashboard was very similar to that of the earlier 1967 Mustangs. It featured a round, hooded **tachometer** and speedometer and even used the same number font as before. Only Mustang enthusiasts would recognize these hints from the past. For a new generation of drivers, the 2005 Mustang looked like a brand-new design.

The fifth-generation 2005 Mustang borrowed the fastback rear-window style and taillights from the 1965–66 models.

Mustang goes retro

Ford's group vice president of global design, J. Mays, designed the fifth-generation Mustang. His style is called "retrofuturism." This means he created new designs by taking older styles and giving them a futuristic twist. So the fifth-generation Mustangs resembled the first-generation. The resemblance was deliberate—the retro look had sold so well in the fourth generation that Ford decided to continue with this winning formula.

External similarities

On the outside, the fifth generation shared styling hints from Mustangs produced between 1965 and 1969. The new Mustang had round headlights that closely resembled those of the 1967–69 models. Prominent wheel fenders popped out from the body as they had in the 1965 Mustang.

New strength

The newly designed chassis was the stiffest one yet, making the structure of the car stronger than ever before. The Mustang's wheelbase was almost six inches (15 cm) longer. The extra length gave the pony car better handling and reduced noise. It also made the Mustang safer to drive.

It may have resembled older Mustangs on the outside, but in terms of performance the fifth-generation Mustang was a brand-new vehicle.

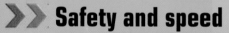
The fifth-generation Mustang had a retro look. It enjoyed a brand-new style but still incorporated hints from first-generation Mustangs.

Safety and speed

The front of the car was designed to be safer, too, if the vehicle should ever find itself involved a head-on collision. The engine was also all new. Mustang's standard 3.6-liter V6 engine was updated with a four-liter SOHC (single overhead camshaft) V6 engine, which gave it an **acceleration** of 0 to 60 mph (97 km/h) in five seconds.

A new generation of fans

Americans liked the new generation. Altogether, the new retro look and the upgraded performance meant strong sales for the fifth-generation Mustang. In its debut year alone (2005), Ford sold over 160,000 Mustangs.

Vital Statistics

2005 Mustang

Production years: 2005
No. built: 160,975
Top speed: 150 mph (241 km/h)
Engine type: Single overhead camshaft (SOHC) V6
Engine size: 244 ci (4.0 liter), 210 hp
Cylinders: 6
Transmission: 5-speed manual or 5-speed automatic
CO_2 emissions: 9.3 tons/yr
EPA fuel economy ratings: 17 mpg (city); 26 mpg (highway)
Price: US$19,215

Hau Thai-Tang

Hau Thai-Tang was born in Saigon, South Vietnam. He first saw a Mustang racecar at a United States Overseas racing tour. He knew then that he wanted to work on Mustangs. He moved to New York City with his family when he was nine years old. He earned his degree in engineering and started work at Ford in 1988. He was chosen as Mustang's chief engineer for the 2005 model.

Even as a young boy living in Vietnam, Hau Thai-Tang knew he wanted to work on Ford Mustangs. He was to become the chief engineer for the 2005 Mustang.

Anniversary Mustang

In 2009, the Mustang reached its forty-fifth birthday. Ford celebrated by redesigning its pony car to make it even safer. It was already known as one of the safest vehicles in its class, but it became even more so in 2009, when side airbags were issued as standard on every Mustang.

Glass roofs

New options for the Mustang coupe and GT models included tinted glass roof panels. People seated inside the vehicle could see above and all around them. The tinted glass saved 20 percent of the energy used for air conditioning. It also protected the interior of the Mustang from fading. It was a pricey option, though—costing buyers almost US$2,000 extra.

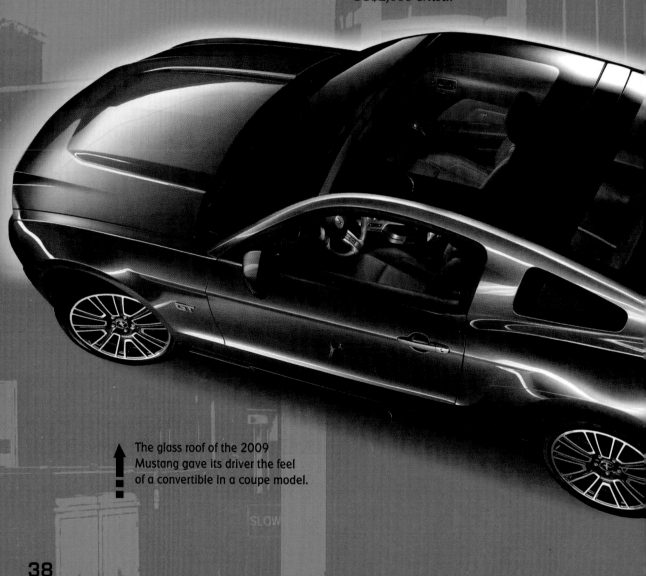

The glass roof of the 2009 Mustang gave its driver the feel of a convertible in a coupe model.

Moody Mustangs

New interior ambient lighting was also offered in 2009. The driver could create a mood by changing the color of lighting in the front and rear footwells and in the front cupholders. These areas could be lit up in any one of seven colors: red, orange, blue, indigo, violet, green, or yellow.

Warriors in Pink Mustangs featured the galloping-pony logo, but for this special edition it runs on top of a pink ribbon.

Warriors in Pink

Ford Mustangs raised money to help cure breast cancer by selling special-edition Warriors in Pink Mustangs in 2008 and 2009. The special Mustang came in black, metallic silver, or white, with pink striping details and pink stitching on the leather seats, steering wheel, and floor mats. Ford hoped to raise half a million U.S. dollars with their Warriors in Pink Mustangs.

39

Chapter 5
Specialty Mustangs ≫≫≫≫≫≫≫

In addition to the standard Mustang models, Ford has always offered a variety of engines, options, and high-performance models. Mustangs have also paced races and raised money for charities. With so many styles, colors, and options to choose from, it's easy to understand why Mustang has always been one of America's most-driven pony cars.

Performance cars

Throughout their life, standard Mustangs such as the coupe and GT models may have been better sellers, but the high-performance Mustangs—the Shelby Cobras and Mach nameplates—have got the reputation of being some of the fastest vehicles on American roads.

Mustang's first outing as a pace car at the Indy 500 came in 1964, with one of the very first of the cars.

Pace cars

A pace car is a specially chosen vehicle that slows racecars down during a race if there is a caution period. Caution periods are called when there has been an accident or when conditions on the racetrack are unsafe. The pace car holds racers' places, and racecars cannot pass other vehicles during the caution period. When the pace car leaves the track the race continues.

It is an honor to be chosen as the official pace car for a race because many people watch these competitions. Throughout its history, the Mustang has paced many important races.

Indy 500

The Indianapolis 500—often called the Indy 500—is an annual 500-mile (805-km) American car race held in Indiana. Mustang was first honored as the race's official pace car in 1964—the car's very first year! The actual pace car, a white Mustang with a blue racing stripe, was equipped with a modified high-performance engine. Ford produced over 200 look-alike pace editions to either sell or give away in dealer promotions.

Pace-car replicas

The next time a Mustang performed as a pace car for the Indy 500 was in 1979, when Ford released the third-generation Mustang. Over 10,000 Mustang pace-car **replicas** were produced to mark the occasion. The silver metallic cars featured running-pony **decals**, red and orange striping, and Indy pace car letter stickers.

1994 special

Mustang returned as the Indy 500 pace car in another generation-debut year. This time it was the fifth-generation car in 1994, and the Mustang Cobra received the honor. Ford offered 1,000 Rio Red SVT Cobra convertible special-edition pace cars for sale to the public. The car was decorated with special pace-car decals, too.

Bulking up

When it was first released, the Mustang was a sporty-looking small car. Lee Iacocca wanted to change the Mustang's image and reputation to that of a more muscular car with gutsier performance and speed. To do this, he had a new line of specialty Mustangs created. They didn't sell as many as the standard lineup of Mustangs, but they did what Iacocca wanted them to—they gave the Mustang's image a burst of interest as well as power.

The 2011 Mustang GT got its first chance to pace the 2011 Daytona 500 race. The special Daytona 500 is painted racing red with the patriotic red, white, and blue stripe down the center of the car.

In 1994, the Mustang Cobra was chosen to pace the Indy 500. It was a red convertible driven by the 1963 Indy-winning racecar driver Parnelli Jones.

A steed for every need

"A Steed for Every Need" was the Mustang's marketing catchphrase, thought up in 1969. It meant that there was a Mustang for every kind of car-buyer. It also appealed to muscle-car enthusiasts, who started buying the lightning-fast specialty vehicles that started coming out in 1967.

Pacing Daytona

The 2011 GT Mustang was the official pace car for the fifty-second Daytona 500. It was red with a red, white, and blue racing stripe down the center of the car. Just before the race, the car was auctioned off to raise money for charity. It was sold for US$300,000, and the proceeds went to the Juvenile Diabetes Research Foundation. Only 50 replicas were produced to sell.

Shelby Mustangs

Carroll Shelby, who has long been the mastermind behind the high-performance Mustang, led the design team from Mustang's early days. In 1965, he and his team took 500 Wimbledon White Mustang fastbacks and modified them with high-performance 289 ci (4.7 liter), 271 hp V8 engines. They were officially equipped to race in the Sports Car Club of America (SCCA) racing competition.

Carroll Shelby

Carroll Shelby raised chickens before he became a racecar driver. When he quit racing he started designing racecars. He started his own company, Shelby American, in 1962, and created his own Shelby Cobra racecar. It had a European chassis but was powered by a high-performance Ford V8 engine. He was hired by Ford in 1964 to design a new line of production Mustangs called Shelby Mustangs.

Former racecar driver Carroll Shelby started designing racecars in the 1960s. The first GT350 Shelby Mustang came out in 1965.

In 1966, Ford gave Hertz 1,000 Shelby GT350H Mustangs, produced the same year, to use as rental cars.

The GT350

Every GT350 built in 1965 was white with blue racing stripes. Race-ready versions came without a back seat to reduce weight. In 1966, more colors were offered for the GT350. The race-ready, street-legal car was considered pretty expensive and had a US$5,995 price tag, which would be worth about US$44,000 today.

The Hertz Rent-A-Racer

In 1966, Ford got together with the car rental company Hertz and created the Rent-A-Racer program. They hoped to boost the sales of the specialty GT Shelby Mustangs. The cars had the same styling as 1966 Shelby Mustangs but were black with gold race stripes and **rocker-panel** details.

Forty years later, in 2006, Ford and Carroll Shelby produced 500 retro GT-H Shelby Mustangs for Hertz car rentals once again. Like the original 1966 GT-H Mustang, the newer model was black with gold stripes and rocker-panel details.

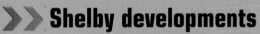

Shelby developments

The 1967 Shelby Mustangs looked quite different from regular Mustangs. They had longer fiberglass front ends and rear spoilers. This was also the year that the GT500 was added to the lineup. The GT500 came equipped with a 355 hp, 428 ci (seven-liter) big-block V8 engine. Two years later, Carroll Shelby stopped designing high-performance production Mustangs for Ford. He rejoined the Ford team in 2006, for Mustang's fifth generation, with a new lineup of Mustang GT500s.

In 1968, Shelby Mustangs included the GT500KR, which came with the Cobra Jet V8 engine. The letters "KR" stood for "King of the Road."

AMAZING FACTS

Shelby sues Ford

Shelby sued Ford when it called its 1984½ twentieth-anniversary edition Mustang the G.T.350. Shelby owned the rights to the name. Instead of renaming the car, Ford decided to pay Shelby to be allowed to use it.

Comeback king

Ford celebrated another forty-year anniversary in 2007, when the Shelby Mustang GT500KR made its return. This time it had a much faster engine than its 1968 relative. The 2007 King of the Road Mustang came with a 540 hp **supercharged** 5.4-liter V8 engine. Only 1,000 were built in 2008. At the time it was the most powerful production Mustang ever built.

The 2008 GT500KR Mustang was equipped with a supercharged V8 engine. It could do 0 to 60 mph (97 km/h) in 4.5 seconds.

Vital Statistics

Shelby GT500KR

Production years: 2008
No. built: 1,000
Top speed: 155 mph (249 km/h)
Engine type: Supercharged DOHC V8
Engine size: 330 ci (5.4 liter), 540 hp
Cylinders: 8
Transmission: 6-speed manual
CO_2 emissions: 11.6 tons/yr
EPA fuel economy ratings: 14 mpg (city); 20 mpg (highway)
Price: US$80,000

Mustang's starring role

In 1968, the Mustang played a starring role in the crime-thriller movie *Bullitt*. The Highland Green 1968 Mustang GT-390 fastback was driven by Detective Frank Bullitt, played by Steve McQueen. The original movie Mustang had a modified engine that gave it greater speed.

In the movie, there is a car-chase scene that many say is one of Hollywood's best. Detective Bullitt is chasing one of the bad guys through the hilly streets of San Francisco. The chase is filmed as though the viewer is in the back seat of Bullitt's Mustang.

The Mustang Bullitt came back in 2001 as a special-edition Mustang Bullitt GT and returned again in 2008 and 2009.

↑ The Mustang Boss 351 succeeded the two original Bosses of 1969 and 1970. It came out for one year only, 1971.

Modern Bullitts

The original Mustang Bullitt was not a special edition. In 2001, however, Ford released a special-edition Mustang Bullitt. These cars featured the same dark-green paint and high-performance driving package that the original had. As a limited special edition, only 5,600 Mustang Bullitts were produced. They sold out quickly!

Bossy Mustangs

The muscle-car-era Mustangs of the 1960s were tougher, bigger, meaner-looking, and meaner-performing cars. In 1969 and 1970, Ford brought out two muscular Mustangs called Bosses. Even their names, Boss 302 and Boss 429, made it sound like these cars were calling all the shots on the road!

Racecars on the road

Both Bosses were street-legal racecars. The Boss 302 participated in the Trans Am racing series. It came with a high-performance small-block 302 V8. The Boss 429 was used for NASCAR racing. It came with a very powerful, high-performance 429 big-block engine. The cars were designed by Larry Shinoda, who had previously worked for General Motors. The Boss 302 was the more popular of the two, selling more than 6,000 cars in 1970. The Boss 429 was too powerful for everyday driving and only sold 499 cars in 1970.

Both Bosses were fired in 1971, and a new Boss 351 fastback replaced them. It wasn't as fast as the other Mustang Bosses, but it was the fastest Mustang built in 1971. This was also the last year for the Boss Mustangs.

The first Mustang Mach 1 was released in 1969. It was a special performance model of the first-generation Mustangs.

Mach 1 Mustangs

The first Mach 1 Mustang came out in 1969. It offered deluxe comfort, with high-backed bucket seats and interior woodgrain detailing. On the outside, Mach 1s were often equipped with **shaker scoops**—metal coverings over an air duct that led to the engine. They were called this because the covering actually shook when the engine was on. The cars could also be recognized by their side stripes and Mach 1 lettering.

Mach 1s were discontinued after 1973. The name was used once for second-generation Mustangs, from 1974 to 1978, but only to describe a special performance package.

AMAZING FACTS

Bond Mach

In 1971, the Mach 1 landed a starring role in the James Bond 007 movie "Diamonds Are Forever." In the movie, James Bond—played by actor Sean Connery—drives a Mach 1 Mustang. It's filmed doing a two-wheeled stunt during a chase scene.

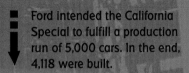

Ford intended the California Special to fulfill a production run of 5,000 cars. In the end, 4,118 were built.

Back to Mach

Ford returned with a special-edition Mach 1 Mustang in 2003 and 2004. These cars, called New Edge Mach 1s, had retro-looking interior seats as well as a retro shaker scoop and a three-level hood, just like the original Mach 1s. Under the hood, though, this was an entirely different car—with a direct overhead camshaft (DOHC) 305 hp V8 engine.

California Special

In 1968, Mustang came out with a special-edition Mustang called the California Special. It had styling features from the Shelby Mustangs but not the same high performance. It was sold only in California. An anniversary edition California Special Mustang returned from 2007 to 2009 and again in 2011.

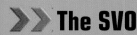

The SVO

In 1981, Ford put together a special group of designers and engineers to work on higher-performance Ford vehicles and racecars. The group was called Special Vehicle Operations, or SVO. In 1984, this team unveiled the Mustang SVO. This high-performance car had European styling and a turbocharged four-cylinder 200 hp engine.

Cobra R

In 1993, Ford's Special Vehicle Team (formerly the SVO) released the Cobra R. A Mustang Cobra is a high-performance Mustang. The "R" stands for racing edition. The Cobra R came with larger brakes and no back seat. It did not have air conditioning or a stereo. Only 107 were produced in 1993. Other Cobra Rs were produced in 1995 and 2000.

Even though it's a street-legal Mustang, the Cobra R's performance is better suited to the racetrack.

The SVT

In 1993, the group was reorganized and renamed the Special Vehicles Team (SVT). They released the high-performance Mustang Cobra and, during some years, the even higher-performance, race-ready Cobra Rs. The team works on other high-performance Ford vehicles, too, including the 2005–06 Ford GT, the Raptor truck, and the Shelby Cobra GT-500 from 2007.

The 2003 SVT Cobra Mustang was equipped with a supercharged V8 engine. It could do 0 to 60 mph (97 km/h) in 4.5 seconds.

Vital Statistics

SVT Cobra Terminator

Production years: 2003–04
No. built: 13,476
Top speed: 155 mph (249 km/h)
Engine type: DOHC modular V8 with Eaton supercharger
Engine size: 281 ci (4.6 liter), 390 hp
Cylinders: 8
Transmission: Tremec T56 6-speed manual
CO_2 emissions: 11.6 tons/yr
EPA fuel economy ratings: 14 mpg (city); 20 mpg (highway)
Price: US$38,000

The Terminator

The SVT team produced a tenth-anniversary SVT Cobra nicknamed Terminator in 2003 and 2004. The name came from the futuristic cyborg character played by Arnold Schwarzenegger in the 1984 movie "The Terminator." This special-edition SVT Cobra came with a 390-hp V8 engine with an Eaton supercharger. In 2003, the Terminator was the most powerful production Mustang ever built!

Chapter 6

Driving Into the Future

For over 45 years, Mustang has had the reputation of being the greatest pony car in America. More Americans have driven a Mustang than any other American sports car. The reasons behind this are many. Ford's promise to keep the Mustang affordable while delivering top performance keeps Americans in the driver's seat.

Since they were first released in 1964, Mustangs have been the car of choice for many Americans.

A car for all

Mustang makes a car to suit almost everyone's driving needs. "A steed for every need" still rings true even after all these years. The fifth generation's new retro look has also persuaded many from the baby-boomer generation who once owned first-generation Mustangs to come back and buy a Mustang once again.

Affordable luxury

The Mustang's base model is priced affordably enough to put drivers in its seats. For those who need more muscle behind their pony, high-performance engines and special-edition Mustangs can satisfy any speed enthusiast with a little more money to spend. Mustang even offers the most horsepower for the best gas mileage for those more concerned with fuel efficiency.

Mustang Club of America

The Mustang Club of America is an organization for Mustang enthusiasts. It began in 1976, at Stone Mountain Park, Georgia. When the club first started out, only owners of Mustang models ranging from 1964½ to 1973 were allowed to join. In 1986, the club changed its rules and allowed owners of any model Mustang to join.

Club members pay a yearly membership fee. The club publishes a monthly magazine called *Mustang Times*. In its 2011 edition, Ford even offers a special Mustang Club of America package, which includes a special dark stainless-steel **billet grille** and side stripe.

 Several 2011 models are available, including a special-edition Mustang Club of America package offered in a V6 coupe or a convertible option.

Fuel-friendly Mustang

The 2011 Mustang V6 is the most fuel-efficient Mustang ever produced. A team tested it on the Bristol Motor Speedway in Tennessee to see how far it could go on one tank of gas. The car set a record. Using fuel-efficient driving techniques, the Mustang averaged close to 48.5 mpg.

2011 Mustang

New engines were introduced to the Mustang lineup for 2011. All basic Mustangs now come with a new V6 engine. This engine is lighter than earlier ones; its block is aluminum instead of the standard cast-iron engine casing. It is also smaller than previous engines, at 227 ci (3.7-liter) with 305 hp. The Mustang GT edition also comes equipped with a new engine, called the Coyote. This is a 412 hp, 302 ci (five-liter) V8 engine.

Shelby GT500 Mustangs got an engine upgrade, too. This model's 330 ci (5.4-liter) engine block is also made of aluminum and weighs over 100 pounds (46 kg) less than the cast-iron block engine. The GT500 engine is listed at 550 hp. Ford has also announced the return of the Boss 302—as the Boss 302R.

Vital Statistics

2011 Mustang

Production years: 2011
No. built: Still in production
Top speed: 160 mph (257 km/h)
Engine type: DOHC V6 aluminum construction
Engine size: 227 ci (3.7 liter), 305 hp
Cylinders: 6
Transmission: 6-speed manual (standard), 6-speed automatic (optional)
CO_2 emissions: 8.5 tons/yr
EPA fuel economy ratings: 19 mpg (city); 29 mpg (highway)
Price: US$23,000

The 2011 Mustang can travel from 0 to 60 mph (97 km/h) in 5.1 seconds.

The interior of the 2011 edition Mustang—summing up the affordable luxury that has appealed to drivers for generations.

Winning awards

Mustang is a car worth talking about, with awards and achievements from its very beginnings. In 1965, the already famous pony car was awarded the Tiffany & Co. Gold Medal award for excellence in American Design. It was the first time a car had received this award.

The Mustang has also collected the more standard car awards, such as being listed as *Motor Trend*'s Car of the Year. *Motor Trend* is an American car magazine that has been published since 1949. Its Car of the Year award is only given to a car with a brand-new design. The Mustang won this award in 1974 for its second generation. It won again in 1994 for the fourth-generation Mustang.

Safety first

All 2011 Mustangs come with the MyKey system. An owner can have separate keys for additional drivers that are coded with specific driving limits. With MyKey, the car owner can limit the vehicle's speed and even audio volume. An owner can make sure that the traction-control system remains on. If seat belts are not done up, it will mute the audio system and remind the driver and passengers to buckle up!

The Mustang has even won awards across the North American border in Canada. In 2005, it was chosen as Canadian Car of the Year in the Best New Sports/Performance Car category.

Mustang museums

Anything as long lasting and popular as the Ford Mustang deserves to be cherished and viewed in a museum. In fact, there are several museums that show off the classic American pony car, although there isn't a museum dedicated solely to the Ford Mustang.

Henry Ford Museum

The Henry Ford Museum is much more than a tribute to the Mustangs, but the car does make an appearance there. The very first Mustang to ever come off the assembly line has its home at the Henry Ford Museum.

Shelby Museum

The Shelby Museum is located in Las Vegas, beside the Las Vegas Speedway. It features the many car designs that Carroll Shelby has worked on during his career—including the Shelby Mustangs. The museum houses antique and new Shelby cars that span several decades, from 1962 to today. There's also a library, gift shop, and Shelby café!

Mustangs are exhibited in museums all over North America. This 1968 Cobra is in the Gilmore Car Museum, in Michigan.

Mustang's legacy

A legacy is a gift from the past that represents the times from which it came. The Ford Mustang is an American legacy that mirrors the economic and fashion trends of Americans from 1964 to today. In its many base and specialty models, it is an American sports car that has truly become a legend.

The future for Mustang

As the Mustang's fiftieth anniversary draws closer, the excitement builds. What will the next-generation Mustang look like? How will it perform? Nobody at this point knows for sure, but you can bet that it will be the best in American design and engineering. It will be affordable, with options to suit everyone's needs. It will be exactly what Americans are looking for in a sports car—just as it has always been.

▚ AMAZING FACTS

Sold by mistake

The first Mustang to come off the assembly line was shipped off to tour Canada. An airline pilot named Stanley Tucker saw the car at a Ford dealership and bought it. The problem was that it was not supposed to be sold! Ford bought it back almost two years later.

■ The Mustang started out as a legend over 45 years ago, and the legend still runs strong today.

Mustang Timeline

1964 The first Mustangs roll of the production line at Dearborn, Michigan

1965 Ford produces over 681,000 Mustangs; the car makes its first movie appearance in *Goldfinger*

1966 Ford and Hertz start the Rent-A-Racer program

1967 Mustang sales decline as other companies enter the pony-car race; Shelby's GT500 is added to the Mustang lineup

1968 Eight different engine options are available in the Mustang; Bunkie Knudsen becomes president of Ford; Mustang appears in the movie *Bullitt*

1969 The Mustang receives a style makeover; two Boss Mustangs are released

1970 Lee Iacocca is made president of the Ford Motor Company

1971 Mach 1 stars in the Bond film *Diamonds Are Forever*

1973 The OPEC oil embargo causes fuel prices in America to skyrocket

1974 The Mustang logo is redesigned to show the horse trotting rather than galloping

1977 Lee Iacocca leaves Ford

1979 A second oil crisis hits America; third generation of Mustangs begins; Mustang paces the Indy 500

1984 The Mustang SVO is released

1989 Work begins on the new Mustang generation, originally called SN95

1992 Mustang sales slip to an all-time low; production moves to Flat Rock, Michigan

1993 Ford releases the Cobra R

1994 Fourth-generation Mustangs are unveiled

1996 A special Mystic Mustang is offered; the new OHC engine is introduced

1999 Mustang celebrates its thirty-fifth anniversary with the New Edge design

2001 The Mustang Bullitt is released as a special edition

2003 The three-millionth Mustang is produced at Dearborn; the new Mach 1 is produced

2004 The Dearborn plant closes its doors

2007 Return of the Shelby Mustang GT500KR

2008 Ford releases the limited-edition Warriors in Pink model in aid of breast cancer

2009 Mustangs are offered with glass roofs and mood lighting

2011 The anniversary California Special is released

Further Information

Books

The Mustang Dynasty
by John M. Clor
(T-5 Design, 2007)

Ford Mustang: Forty Years of Fun
(Consumer Guide Publications International, Ltd., 2004)

Mustang: An American Classic
by Mike Mueller
(Universe Publishing, 2009)

Web sites

www.ford.com/
The official web site of the Ford Motor Company

www.hfmgv.org/museum/index.aspx
The web site for the Henry Ford Museum in Dearborn, Michigan

www.shelbyautos.com/index.asp
The web site for Shelby American Inc., with information about
Mustang mastermind Carroll Shelby and his cars

Glossary

acceleration A measure of how quickly a vehicle speeds up

acronym A word that is made by using the first letter from a number of words

aerodynamic Describing a shape that is designed to move easily through wind at high speed

billet grille A grille with a special covering that allows air to flow in while preventing road debris from entering the grille

bucket seats Car seats that are molded to accommodate one person, as opposed to flat bench seats

chassis A car's frame or platform

concept car A vehicle made to show the public a new design or technology

coupe A hard-topped sports car with two seats

decals Stickers with pictures or lettering used to decorate a car

embargo A governmental policy that bans trade with a particular country

emblem A figure or object used to represent an organization

emissions Substances—usually harmful—that escape into the air, for example from vehicle exhausts

executives People in senior management positions at a company

export Something that is traded from one country to another

fastback A style of car whose roofline slopes down continuously at the back

grille The front screen of a vehicle; it usually sits between the headlights

horsepower (hp) The amount of pulling power an engine has, calculated as the number of horses it would take to pull the same load

mass-produced Manufactured in large quantities, often using assembly lines

muscle car A high-performance two-door car with a big, beefy engine

notchback A style of car in which there is a sharp vertical drop from the roof to the rear

production car A car that is made in large numbers on an assembly line

recession A period of time when the economy is not doing well

replicas Copies identical to the original

retro Relating to a re-creation of a fashion of the past, often in an updated manner

rocker panels The parts of the car that run underneath the doors from wheel to wheel

shaker scoop A component on the hood of a car covering an air duct that allows air to flow directly into the engine compartment

supercharged Referring to the use of an air compressor for the forced induction of an internal combustion engine

surveying Questioning a group of people to see what they like or dislike

tachometer An instrument on a vehicle's dashboard that displays the rotations per minute (rpm) of the engine's shaft

torque A force that causes something to rotate or turn; in a car, the power that an engine generates by turning

turbocharged Of an engine, fitted with a gas compressor to make the vehicle it powers go faster

Index

Entries in **bold** indicate pictures